EVERYDAY PRAYERS FOR EVERYDAY PEOPLE

Also by Stephen W. Hiemstra:

A Christian Guide to Spirituality

Una Guía Cristiana a la Espiritualidad

Oraciones

Prayers

Life in Tension

Prayers of a Life in Tension

Called Along the Way

Spiritual Trilogy

EVERYDAY PRAYERS FOR EVERYDAY PEOPLE

Stephen W. Hiemstra

T2PNEUMA PUBLISHERS LLC
CENTREVILLE, VIRGINIA

EVERYDAY PRAYERS FOR EVERYDAY PEOPLE

Copyright © 2018 Stephen W. Hiemstra.

All rights reserved. With the exception of short excerpts used in articles and critical review, no part of this work may be reproduced, transmitted, or stored in any form whatsoever, printed or electronic, without prior written permission of the publisher.

T2Pneuma Publishers LLC
P.O. Box 230564, Centreville, Virginia 20120
www.T2Pneuma.com

Names: Hiemstra, Stephen W., author.
Title: Everyday prayers for everyday people / Stephen W. Hiemstra.
Description: Centreville, VA: T2Pneuma Publishers LLC, 2018.
Identifiers: ISBN 978-1942199229 (Hardcover) | 978-1942199342 (Kindle) | 978-1942199595 (ePub) | LCCN 2018910348
Subjects: LCSH: Prayers. | Christian life. | BISAC: RELIGION / Christian Life / Prayer
Classification: LCC BV245 .H52 2018 |DDC 242.8–dc23

Edited by Reid Satterfield.

All Scripture quotations, unless otherwise indicated, are taken from The Holy Bible, English Standard Version, Copyright © 2000; 2001 by Crossway Bibles, a division of Good News Publishers. Used by permission. All rights reserved.

Gratefully acknowledge permission to use the following:

Prayers blogged (http://www.T2Pneuma.net) from September 2016 through September 2018.

Threadpainting; *"Sisters"* (2005) by Sharron Deacon Begg of Guelph, Ontario, Canada. http://threadpaintersart.blogspot.com.

Cover design by SWH

CONTENTS

PRESENCE
1. Presence.. 2
2. Against Entropy....................................... 3
3. Disappointment..................................... 4
4. Full Presence...5
5. Fruits of the Spirit................................. 6

FAITH
6. Steady Hand.. 10
7. Prayer Journey...................................... 11
8. Discernment.. 12
9. Cloudy Days.. 13
10. Potter.. 14
11. A Risk-Manager's Prayer......................15
12. Faith..16
13. Prosper Faith....................................... 17
14. Dialogue... 18
15. Love.. 19
16. Today..20
17. Transcendence......................................21
18. Forgiveness... 22

CHURCH
19. Baptism..24
20. Faith of the Newly Baptized................25
21. Confessional..26
22. Stewardship.. 27
23. Reconciliation..................................... 28
24. Passion for Missions...........................30
25. Collect for a God Who Listens........... 32
26. New Churches.................................... 33
27. Evangelists... 34
28. Beginning and Ending.........................35

Contents - v

29. Unity..36
30. Prayers of the People...................................... 37

SABBATH REST
31. Rest... 40
32. Congruity..41
33. Thanks for Restoration....................................42
34. Quiet Times..43
35. Peace..44
36. Shalom...46
37. Self-Care.. 48

ADORATION
38. Holy Spirit... 50
39. Memories...51
40. All Forgiving Lord.. 52
41. Praise... 54
42. Giving Thanks.. 55
43. Adoration...56

HEALING
44. Healing from Sin.. 58
45. Healing...59
46. Casting Out Dark Shadows.............................61
47. Healing, Comfort, and Deliverance................. 63
48. Co-Dependence.. 65

HOLIDAYS
49. New Year's 2017... 68
50. Lent.. 69
51. Lent 2018... 71
52. Church Workers at Easter............................... 72
53. Easter...73
54. Mom..74

55. Mother's Day 2018 75
56. Father's Day 76
57. Thanksgiving 77
58. Evangelists 78
59. Advent 2016 79
60. Advent 2017 80
61. Christmas 2016 81
62. Christmas 2017 82

FAMILY
63. Family 84
64. Family 2017 85
65. Kids 86
66. Elderly Parents 87

INTERCESSION
67. Election 2016 90
68. Innocent Students 92
69. Silent People 93
70. Teachers 95
71. Persecution 96
72. Authors 98
73. Comfort for Those Alone 99
74. Those in Peril 100
75. Memory Impaired 102
76. Traveling Mercies 103

SEASONS
77. Open Doors 106
78. January 107
79. Tulips 108
80. Spring 109
81. Summer 110
82. When Daylight Fades 111
83. Attentiveness 113

Contents - vii

84. Autumn.. 115
85. Winter..116
86. Stillness of Winter... 117

LAMENTATIONS
87. Covering Prayer...120
88. When We are Alone.. 121
89. Dimmer Lights... 122
90. Grief.. 123
91. Cooler Weather... 126

STRENGTH
92. Workouts... 128
93. Thanks for Quiet Days...................................... 130
94. Doldrums... 131
95. Solitude.. 132
96. Relief... 133
97. Strength... 134
98. Vindication..136
99. Living Water... 138

ABOUT... 139

PRESENCE

1. Presence

Heavenly Father,

We praise you for your quiet presence—
sustaining all creation and
nurturing it with your love.

Though darkness surrounds us and
the fear of death overwhelms us,
you cover us with the blood of Christ—
your hedge of everlasting protection.

Cover our sin when our judgment lapses
and we cannot admit our transgressions,
even to ourselves.

Thankfully,
you are the Almighty One—
you do not share our weaknesses and
we can rely in your goodness,
even when we walk alone down dark paths.

In the power of your Holy Spirit,
grant us strength to model
your presence and goodness
to those around us.

In Jesus' precious name, Amen

1/28/2018

2. Against Entropy

Most Merciful Father,

I praise you
for your unchanging character,
your immutability in the face of erosion, pain, and death—
for your love conquers all,
from the sting of war
to the impurity of common dust
that brings disease, biting insects, and filth.

I confess
that I pale in the presence of even tiny obstacles and
fear is my constant companion.

Forgive
my timidity and cowardliness,
as strength fails me.

In the power of your Holy Spirt,
instill in me your wisdom and
strength to face the day
that I might minister to those around me and
find the courage to live the life that you intended.

In Jesus precious name, Amen.

8/12/2018

3. Disappointment

Heavenly Father, Beloved Son, Spirit of Truth,

All praise and honor be unto you,
Lord of my coming and going,
the one whom I can truly trust.

I confess that some days my heart is broken and
none but you will do—
for my sins are too numerous and
my trust in others is too fleeting for my heart to bear.

Thank you for giving me a new day and
for bearing me up
so that I can face new trials and
know that you are closer than my beating heart.

Be my North Star once again.

In the power of your Holy Spirit,
grant me strength for the day,
grace for those I meet, and
peace.

In Jesus precious name, Amen.

7/22/2018

4. *Full Presence*

Almighty, Ever-present Father,

I praise you for your constant presence in my life.

For neither death nor life, nor angels nor rulers,
nor things present nor things to come,
nor powers, nor height nor depth,
nor anything else in all creation,
will be able to separate me from your love
through Jesus Christ. (Rom 8:38–39)

But I confess that I have trouble being fully present
in the lives of the people around me—
too often I am tired, distracted, and inattentive,
not reflecting your example.

Nevertheless, I give thanks
that you are patient with me and
speak gently to me even when I stray.

In the power of your Holy Spirit,
teach me once again what I must do and
grant me the strength to do it.

May your grace shine through me and
may I experience the peace
that passes all understanding. (Phil 4:7)

In Jesus' precious name, Amen.

7/29/2018

5. Fruits of the Spirit

Almighty Father, Beloved Son, Ever-Present Spirit,

I praise you
for your model of a life well-lived
in your son, our savior, Jesus Christ.

May his example remain ever-present before my eyes,
his voice ever-sounding in my ears, and
the touch of his hand ever-warming my shoulder.

I confess
that I am too easily seduced
by the works of the flesh—
*"sexual immorality, impurity, sensuality,
idolatry, sorcery, enmity, strife, jealousy,
fits of anger, rivalries, dissensions, divisions,
envy, drunkenness, orgies, and things like these."*
(Gal 5:19–21)

They are continuously before my eyes in the media and
I am slow to turn my head in revulsion—
forgive my sloth.

I give thanks
that you are a God of
second, third, and fourth chances—
may I soon stop trying your patience.

I ask Lord,
kindle in me the fruits of your spirit—
*"love, joy, peace, patience, kindness, goodness, faithfulness,
gentleness, [and] self-control"* (Gal 5:22–23)

that I might inherit your kingdom and
walk in your ways
all the days of my life.

In Jesus's name, Amen.

9/2/2018

FAITH

6. Steady Hand

Almighty Father,

All glory and honor are yours, Lord,
for you are my fortress and
your presence
like a hand on my shoulder.

Why do I fear; why does my grip falter?

I confess
that my faith hangs by a thread—
for I know that someday my strength will fail and
my only hope is in you.

Thank you
for a new day and
the opportunity to serve in your name.

In the power of your Holy Spirit,
grant me the strength to be the person
you created me to be—
fully present to those around me.

In Jesus' precious name, Amen.

8/5/2018

7. Prayer Journey

Precious Savior,

Stay with me this morning
as the snow is all around me and
I am not sure where to go.

Is it snow or is it just the morning fuzz in my eyes—
fuzz that takes hold of me and
hems me in until I shake it off in the gym?

Stay with me this afternoon
as I wander from task to task and
from chat to chat.

Deepen my thoughts;
raise my awareness; and
help me to become a better companion—
someone helpful on the journey,
not someone just taking up space.

Stay with me this evening
as my strength flags—
even as I frantically desire to push on.

In the power of your Holy Spirit,
grant me the strength and wisdom
to create and cherish and share
before the night takes its toll
and I fade with the light.

In Jesus' precious name, Amen.   9/8/2018

8. Discernment

Loving Father,

I praise you for your loving presence in my life
throughout this year.

For you alone are holy and
stand outside time and space—
I cannot approach you on my own,
but only through your love,
covered by the blood of Jesus
as your draw me unto yourself.

I confess that I have not been a perfect son—
my faith is weak,
my sins are many, and
my iniquities forever parade before my eyes.

Forgive me; teach me to be a more perfect son.

Thank you for the many blessings of this year—
for work completed, relationships deepened,
healings received, and the opportunity for greater service.

In the power of your Holy Spirit,
grant me the heart and mind of Christ,
that my heart will be opened,
my mind renewed, and
my hands strengthened
that I may discern your will more fully and
draw closer to you day by day.

In Jesus' precious name, Amen.   11/26/2017

9. Cloudy Days

Loving Father,

I give special thanks for your presence on cloudy days,
when the rain soaks through my clothes and
the sun shines dimly.

I cherish your presence most when I am cold and
can't remember what it was like to be warm—
maybe the sun really shines, but I can't see it;
maybe the clouds aren't endless, but I can't see it.

Be especially near.

In the power of your Holy Spirit,
protect those I love from my stumbling;
guard my heart from besetting fears and
temptations that overwhelm; and
shield my mind that I do not sin.

So I will know in my heart
that the sun will shine again one day.

In Jesus' precious name, Amen.

11/5/2017

10. Potter

Almighty God, Father of our Lord, Spirit of Truth,

Why have you formed me, all-knowing potter,
the way that you have? (Jer 18:2–7)

In your creative urge, did you have a special use in mind?

Did you mean me for everyday use,
like a pot for baked beans or
maybe a dish for casseroles or a tuna salad?

Are my colors plain to all who see me
even as I am wholly blind?

Did you mean me for a special occasion,
like a Christmas dish
that is highlighted, remembered, and cherished once a year
but spends most days hidden in the closet?

Am I brightly colored, festive, memorable
even if only for a day?

Thank you, Lord, for veiling your purposes from me,
that I may serve as you see fit, each and every day.

In Jesus' name, Amen.

9/24/2017

11. A Risk-Manager's Prayer

Almighty Father,

Forgive me for leaning on insurance policies
rather than trusting in you.

Forgive me for building and filling barns
while children go to bed hungry. (Luke 12:18)

Forgive me for having a hard heart
taking my cues from Pharaoh
when Jesus has shown us a better way. (Matt 6:26)

As the hymnist[1] writes:

Be Thou my Vision, O Lord of my heart
Naught be all else to me, save that Thou art
Thou my best Thought, by day or by night
Waking or sleeping, Thy presence my light.

Oh Lord, shape me more clearly in your image
in spite of my ignorance, selfishness,
greed, and self-pity.

Through the power of your Holy Spirit,
turn my heart to you
that I might live a better way.

In Jesus' name, Amen.

9/17/2017

---

[1] https://en.wikipedia.org/wiki/Be_Thou_My_Vision.

12. Faith

Heavenly Father,

I believe in Jesus Christ,
the son of the living God,
who died for our sins and
was raised from the dead.

Come into my life.

Help me to renounce and grieve the sin in my life
that separates me from you.

Cleanse and renew me
by the power of your Holy Spirit
so that sin's grip will be loosened.

Strengthen my faith—
bring saints and a faithful church into my life
to keep me honest with myself and
draw me closer to you.

Break any chains—
be they pains or sorrows or grievous temptations—
that bind me to the past.

May I freely welcome you into my life,
who through Christ Jesus can bridge any gap and
heal any affliction, now and always.

In Jesus' previous name, Amen.

7/23/2017

13. Prosper Faith

Almighty Father,

I praise you
for the gift of another day,
when the newest of the day (Isa 43:1) can be expressed
in renewed faith.

I confess
that I have too frequently blocked your access to my heart
in despair,
in self-pity, and
in cynicism not worthy of your love.

Thank you for not giving up on me. (Ezek 37)

In the power of your Holy Spirit,
give me a stronger, more vibrant faith (2 Cor 4:8–9),
where I am able to make you Lord
over increasing parts of my life (Acts 4:36–37) and
drain the despair, self-pity, and cynicism,
laying my griefs at your feet. (Ps 31:9–14)

In Jesus' name, the founder and
perfecter of my faith (Heb 12:2), Amen.

5/28/2017

14. Dialogue

Oh dear Lord:

Hear me; answer my prayer—
righteous God in whom I trust—
for you have rescued me from suffering.

I hear you, oh foolish man,
but how long must I endure you shaming me?

How long, oh righteous blowhard,
will you prefer lies to my word?

For I have set my people apart from all this and
hear them when they pray, as I have instructed—
do not sin when you get mad;
reflect quietly on your actions;
trust and worship me with an upright heart.

Do not listen to those who wait only for miracles and
wait for me to bless and lead their every step.

Oh Lord, you fill my life with joy
more than banquets and fine wine.

For in you, my mind is at rest—
I am at ease and
can sleep knowing that I am safe.

In Jesus name, Amen.[1]   3/26/2017

---

1 Inspired by Psalm 4.

15. Love

Heavenly Father,

We praise you for the mercy
that you showed us in sending Jesus Christ,
who died on a cross for us and our salvation.

For in your mercy, we have seen your love—
sacrificial love that carried a price;
covenantal love that keeps a promise;
divine love that bridged the gaps
between the eternal and mortal,
between the holy and the unclean.

Have pity on us, a pitiable people—
people who wink at eternity for a night on the town;
people who spurn holiness for a penny's entertainment.

Thank you for the love of Christ.

In the power of your Holy Spirit,
help us to grow into his love and
share it with those around us.

In Jesus' precious name, Amen.

2/12/2017

16. Today

God of all mercy, Loving Son, Healing Spirit,

We praise you for creating heaven and earth;
all that is, was, or will ever be;
for things seen and unseen.

We thank you for revealing yourself
in the person of Jesus of Nazareth;
who in life was a role model for sinners,
in death became a ransom for sin, and
in new life gave us the hope of salvation.

We look upon the life, death, and
resurrection of Jesus and
see your love for us and
want to praise you.

We thank you for your Holy Spirit;
who is ever close, sustains all things,
provisions all things, and
gives every good gift.

Holy, holy, holy is the Lord of Hosts, the giver of life, and
the redeemer of men and women,
in whom we live and move and
have our being. Amen.

9/18/2016

17. Transcendence

Heavenly Father,

We praise you for your glory—
for you are holy, set apart, and
stand outside of time.

All glory is yours—
for we are sinful, quick to compromise, and
mortally bound to times and places beyond our control.

Do not leave us content to look into the mirror—
to grasp at visceral pleasures, or
to chase after temporal fantasies.

Lift us out of the mire of power politics,
the pit of merchant's wares, and
the icy embrace of superficial inattention.

It is not all about us—
salvation is your gift, not ours;
help us to accept it and live in obedience to you.

Through the power of you Holy Spirit,
remind us of our past;
guide our steps; and
let us live in the hope of the resurrection.

Through Jesus' example and in his name, Amen.

9/25/2016

18. Forgiveness

Blessed Lord Jesus,

We give thanks for your time among us and
the gift of your Holy Spirit.

We give thanks that even from the cross
you forgave our sins,
the ones that placed you there.

Grant us eyes that see and ears that hear
that we might follow your example.

Give us the strength
to recognize our own sins,
to turn from our iniquities, and
to hear your voice
even as other voices scream ever so loudly.

May we testify, not to our truth,
but to your truth
by what we say and
do each passing day.

May the scales fall from our eyes
in the name of the Father, Son, and
Holy Spirit, Amen.

11/13/2016

CHURCH

19. Baptism

Merciful Father,

We praise you for the day of our baptism
when Jesus washed away our sins and
we experienced the miracle of restoration and rebirth.

We confess that our salvation rests on nothing less
than Jesus' death and righteousness.

Forgive our weakness and sin.

We thank you for the many blessings of this life and
the hope that you have given us.

Through the power of your Holy Spirit,
bring us back into communion
with our true selves in Christ.

May we remember our baptism
that our souls would find rest and
advance the day
when you shall come again in victory.

In Jesus´ precious name, Amen.

8/19/2018

20. Faith of the Newly Baptized

Heavenly Father,

Thank you
for the gift of faith
that we were baptized.

Thank you
for your willingness to enter our lives and
recreate us in your image,
in spite of our rebellion and sin.

Thank you
that, through your Holy Spirit,
we can take a small step of faith and
choose a new path,
not knowing where it will lead,
but confident that you will be with us.

Thank you
for washing away our sins
through the blood of the lamb
that we might die to those sins and
be born again in your spirit.

Thank you. Thank you. Thank you.

Through the power of your Holy Spirit,
guard our hearts and minds in Jesus Christ and
grow our faith,
that we might inch closer to you
each passing day. Amen.

7/16/2017

21. Confessional

Almighty Father,

Forgive me for my many sins, iniquities, and trespasses.

For I have fallen short of your goals for my life,
I have failed to do many things that I should have, and
I have broken trust with your gracious laws.

Have mercy on me
through the blood of your son, Jesus Christ,
who though he lived a sinless life
yet was crucified on the cross,
that I might find forgiveness through him.

Hear my prayer and
have compassion on me,
though I am undeserving.

Fill my heart with your Holy Spirit,
that I might be saved and
rest with you eternally.

In Jesus' name, Amen.

12/10/2017

22. Stewardship

Most Generous Father,

We praise you
for your abundant generosity
that was obvious—
in the turning of water into wine at Cana,
in the feeding of the five thousand, and
in the provision of fish to the disciples.

We confess
that we have not always emulated you
in our own dealings with time,
talents, money, or possessions.

We thank you
for remembering us
with health, family, and
numerous blessings.

Forgive our tightfistedness,
our numbness towards the needs of others, and
our willingness to fight for what we think is ours alone.

In the power of your Holy Spirit,
teach us to be godly stewards
of our time, money, and talents, and
to know when enough is enough.

May we reflect the generosity that you have first shown us.

In Jesus' name, Amen.   7/15/2018

23. Reconciliation

Almighty Father,

I praise you
for the suffering and sacrifice of Jesus on the cross,
who reconciled me to you and
made salvation possible
even as I have been slow to accept this reconciliation or
to extend it to those around me
who do not know you.

For if I refuse to be reconciled to you,
I cannot be reconciled with others.

I confess
that I have let feelings of hopelessness and
powerless impede my own efforts
to extend your love to those around me.

Forgive my weakness;
pardon my sin; and
do not let my iniquity define who I am.

I give thanks
for the example of Christ's life, work, and sacrifice; and
for the many blessings of this life—
family, work, health, and the opportunity of ministry.

In the power of your Holy Spirit,
let the spirit of Easter
lie before my eyes, ring in my ears, and
resonate in my heart,
that I might not tarry in inaction

but embrace your love and live into it.

Be especially near to all who suffer.

In Jesus' precious name, Amen.

4/29/2018

24. Passion for Missions

Almighty and Loving Father,

We praise you for the pouring out of your Holy Spirit
to establish the church on the day of Pentecost.

To you and you alone
be the glory and honor,
now and always.

We confess that as your church,
we are broken and sinful,
yet in Christ we are also forgiven.

For your forgiveness, we are truly grateful.

We are also thankful for the many blessings
that you have poured out on us as your people.

For in Christ, we are able to undertake ministry
that would be impossible for us as individuals.

We ask now, Lord, for your strength
to carry on with the mission
that you have given us,
even as your church remains divided and
the world spins ever faster.

As Jesus said:
*"As the Father has sent me,
even so I am sending you."* (John 20:21)

In the power of your Holy Spirit,

protect us from being diverted to other missions and
especially from the spirit of this age
who harries us relentlessly.

In Jesus' precious name, Amen.

7/8/2018

25. Collect for a God Who Listens

Ever Attentive Father,

We praise you
that you care enough to listen,
that your concern for the immigrant, the orphan, and
the widow is foremost (Exod 22:21–27),
even when we focus on our own concerns and
play politics with the welfare of others.

We confess
that we are cold-blooded and
hide behind walls, rules, and policies
that we blame on others
even as we seek our own benefit before offering relief.

Forgive us our deaf ears;
rid us of our addictions; and
heal the wounds
that we have needlessly inflicted on others and
brought on ourselves.

In the power of your Holy Spirit,
give us listening ears
that we might learn from your example
that in our learning we might also share in your salvation.

Through Jesus Christ and in his name, Amen.

7/1/2018

26. New Churches

Heavenly Father,

We praise you for new churches,
small churches that build the family of God
in new places with new people.

Guide our efforts to offer light in a dark world.

Grant us strength,
the grace to love the unloved and
to offer peace where conflict reigns.

In the power of your Holy Spirit,
bless our efforts with living fruit—
light in dark places, prayers lifted up, lives changed, and
joy where none exists.

In Jesus precious name, Amen.

10/29/2017

27. Evangelists

Almighty Father,

I pray for evangelists whose words of faith
can be heard, shared, and responded to.

Pour out your Holy Spirit on all those
who have yet to hear your name,
recognize your voice, or
open up their hearts to receive Christ.

Be especially present with those
whose hearts of stone
have kept them in darkness.

Soften their hearts and our own.

May your voice be heard
even in our incoherent mumbling.

In Jesus' precious name, Amen.

10/15/2017

28. *Beginning and Ending*

Almighty Father,

We praise you
for creating us
male and female in your image,
not for our glory, but yours alone. (Gen 1:27)

We humbly confess
that we have resisted your light and
refused to do good. (Gen 1:3–4)

We give thanks
that in creating heaven and earth
you made your ways abundantly clear (Rom 1:19–20) and
that we might escape the wages of sin and
gain eternal life through your son, Our Redeemer.
(1 Cor 15:3–4)

We beg of you
that we might choose the light and
honor your son
by the power of your Holy Spirit. (John 14:6)

Through Jesus Christ, Our Lord
who is the Alpha and the Omega,
the beginning and the end (Rev 1:8), Amen.

10/1/2017

29. Unity

Gracious Lord of Heaven and Earth,

We give thanks for the many
blessings that we have received;
blessings that are scarce to some and
absent to others;
blessings that may evoke jealousy, envy, and strife.

Give us generous hearts, open eyes, and
outstretched hands,
that all might be blessed by the blessings
we have received from your hands.

We ask for unity.
Grant us the opportunities for reconciliation and
an end to injustice.

May we not gloat;
may we not reject our neighbors; or
hold on too tightly to our own blessings.

Open our eyes to the needs around us;
open our ears to the voices that we have trouble hearing;
give us the patience to listen when others need to speak.

By the power of your Holy Spirit,
bring us together as a nation
that we might follow Jesus' example in all we do—
this day and every day.

And grant us peace in Jesus' precious name, Amen.

11/20/2016

30. Prayers of the People

Almighty God, Beloved Son, Spirit of Truth,

We praise you
for your mercy, compassion, patience,
covenantal love, and truth.

We give thanks
that in your church we receive—
the manifestation of your Holy Spirit,
the nurturing of our faith,
the community of believers,
the opportunity of service, and
a refuge from life's storms.

We confess
that we the church have not listened to your spirit;
we have not always cherished your word;
we have not always been salt and light;
we have not always borne the burden of others or
been a refuge to the weary.

Prepare her for yourself;
revive her faith,
return her to your word,
embolden her witness,
strengthen her in perilous times,
grant her peace in the midst of chaos.

In Jesus' precious name, Amen.

1/22/2017

SABBATH REST

31. Rest

Lord of the Sabbath,

Teach me to rest.

Disconnect me from the Internet;
take away my phone;
transport me off the grid—
that I might rest with you,
that I might be truly present with others, and
that I might once again cherish my time not working.

Calm my nerves;
deliver me from fear;
let me not care what others think—
that I might recognize the man in the mirror,
that I might care for my kids and my parents, and
that I might serve you without reservation.

Forgive my absence in mind and body;
grant me your presence;
fill my empty heart with your Holy Spirit.

Breath life into these bones. (Ezek 37)

In Jesus' precious name, Amen.

5/27/2018

32. Congruity

Merciful Father,

How long must I wait to see your face more clearly—
to feel your hand on my shoulder and
know that I have served you well?

My soul longs to hear your voice above the chaos of life and
to sense your passion over creation.

Be especially present in this time and place.

Open hearts and minds in this desperate land.

Save me from the specter of a life lived poorly,
out of harmony with your will.

In the power of your Holy Spirit,
grant me strength for the day;
grace for those I meet; and
the peace that passes all understanding.

In Jesus' precious name, Amen.

6/3/2018

33. Thanks for Restoration

Heavenly Father,

All praise and honor are yours,
for you are the God who saves,
who restores the downtrodden;
who heals the afflicted.

We confess
that we are riddled with fear and
doubts on the day of affliction and
have trouble seeing a future of health and vitality.

Yet, thanks to you,
even the night passes into day,
the lame walk, and the blind see.

Thanks to you,
our fears are vanquished,
our doubts allayed,
our healing is possible, and
our hope is renewed.

In the power of your Holy Spirit,
strengthen our faith, restore our confidence,
grow ever-nearer,
that we might always rest only in you.

In Jesus' name, Amen

2/18/2018

34. Quiet Times

Precious Lord Jesus:

I give thanks for quiet times—
times of solitude and solace;
times when your presence is especially near;
times when I am overwhelmed; and
you send me for a time-out—
not for punishment,
but for rest.

Without your presence,
the world overwhelms me.

Be especially near
when by myself I just cannot be.

Thank you for quiet times. Amen

2/5/2017

35. Peace

Almighty God,

Grant us shalom, your peace—
more than just the absence of war.

May we never pray for peace
while harboring war in our hearts or
only after we have gotten our way.

Restore us more fully in your likeness
that we might be saved from ourselves,
from greed, from selfishness,
from hardened hearts and stopped ears.

Teach us how to be ashamed;
may we learn again to blush.

Teach us to order our lives by your word
that your ways may be our guide and
your truths our heart's joy.

May your watchman see and
his trumpet be heard
that we might open our eyes and
not stumble into sin and perish.

Forgive the sins of our fathers and
protect our hearts
from the temptation to repeat them
that the day of reckoning
might not come upon us today. (Jer 6:13-23)

In the power of your Holy Spirit,
enter our hearts and cleanse them,
that we might be saved
through Jesus Christ, our Lord. Amen.

8/20/2017

36. Shalom

Wonderful Counselor, Mighty God,
Everlasting Father, Prince of Peace (Isa 9:6),

We praise you
for your example of perfection in the Trinity—
Father, Son, and Holy Spirit,
in communion, in relationship,
working together in love and peace
to sustain, empower, and protect our world.

We thank you
that you are ever-present, ever-enabling us
to become sons and daughters in your family—
the church.

We thank you
for the gift of salvation and the hope of eternal life
available to us through the death and
resurrection of your son, Jesus Christ.

Forgive us
for our indifference to the suffering of the people of Syria;
open our hearts and
correct our ways.

Forgive us
for the prejudices and injustices of our society,
eager to find fault and oblivious to the truth;
open our eyes to our own faults and self-deception.

Forgive us
for the injustices of poverty and illness

among us in a land of plenty;
soften our hearts and open our hands.

Help us
to work out our salvation,
live into our sonship, and
strive for the peace
that passes all understanding
knowing that you will come in glory
to bring us ever-closer to you.

Teach our leaders humility;
teach us to submit to their leadership; and
help us to make room for you in our lives.

Grant us peace in our hearts,
peace in our relationships, and
peace with you.

In Jesus precious name, Amen.

10/9/2016

37. Self-Care

Holy Father,

I praise you for the quiet days,
when I am able to care for myself,
my world seems peaceful, and
my mind is at ease.

Forgive my selfish inability to focus
on the needs of those around me,
the pain and distress of so many others.

I give thanks
that the weight of the world is on your shoulders,
not mine,
because I cannot bear it—
not today, not ever.

For you alone are God.

In the power of the Holy Spirit,
help me to be a faithful servant
in the ways that you made me to be.

In Jesus' name, Amen.

10/8/2017

ADORATION

38. Holy Spirit

Almighty Father,

Praise to you, loving father,
for your infinite wisdom, mercy, power, and grace.

We praise you
because our limits bind us and
our strength often fails—
for we are weak kneed and
our hearts are sick with every manner of vileness.

We yield to the slightest temptation and
bow before idols
that our minds churn out and serve day after day.

But we thank you
for the gift of your Holy Spirit—
to guide our thoughts and calm our hearts
and give us the strength
needed to walk in your ways.

Be our constant companion,
a helper in our daily struggles.

Keep us secure in this turbulent world and
grant us peace in our hearts,
that we may reflect your image
more clearly day by day.

In Jesus' precious name, Amen.

5/20/2018

39. Memories

Beloved Father,

Thank you
for giving me a loving family,
who have always been with me
even when I was sick and irritable and
no fun at all to be with.

Thank you
for placing godly friends in my life,
who have shared my pain and felt my sorrows
more than I can even recall.

Thank you
for the countless blessings
that I mostly took for granted like
the legs that I walk on,
the ears that I hear with, and
the eyes that let me see.

In the power of your Holy Spirit,
help me to be more thankful—
to share other's pains,
to be more loving, and
to share with others your many blessings.

In Jesus' precious name, Amen.

4/15/2018

40. All Forgiving Lord

Almighty Father, Blessed Son, Holy Spirit,

All praise and honor are yours, Lord,
the God of our youth and
the many years since then.

For you forgive our sins,
overlook our transgressions, and
set aside our iniquity
for the sake of your son, Jesus Christ,
who lived a sinless life,
died on the cross for our sins,
rose from the dead, and
reigns with you in glory.

Forgive
our haughty spirit;
our lust for power; and
our worship of money.

May we learn to forgive our neighbors;
those who we do not understand; and
those who make war on us—
not because they deserve our forgiveness,
but because our hearts belong to you and
vengeance is yours alone.

Remember the fallen,
heal our wounds,
comfort the afflicted, and
soften bitter hearts.

For our lives hang in the balance day after day,
solely sustained by your provision,
not through any merit of our own—
may your Holy Spirit rule our hearts.

In the sunshine of your love,
may we replace hate with understanding,
delight in the example of your son, and
grow more like him day by day.

In the warmth of your grace,
grant us—
ears that listen,
eyes that see, and
a heart for those whom you love.

Through the power of your Holy Spirit and
in Jesus' name, Amen.

9/11/2016

41. Praise

Lord Almighty,

All praise and honor be to your name,
the name above all names.

Lord of our comings and goings,
our beginnings and endings, and everything
that we were, are, or will ever be.

For you have shared yourself with us graciously,
through the person of Jesus of Nazareth,
who lived as a perfect example to sinners,
died on the cross for our salvation, and
rose from the dead
that we might have life eternal.

Yet, in spite of our sinful state,
you gave us the Spirit of Truth, the Holy Spirit,
who leads us in every good deed,
provides us with every good gift,
provisions and sustains our world, and
remains with us on good days and bad.

Accept our praise
as we give ourselves to you.

In Jesus' name, Amen.

10/22/2017

42. Giving Thanks

Almighty Father,

We praise you for your compassionate presence,
your redeeming love, and
your boundless blessings.

For we are often—
absent when we are needed,
aloof when we should be available, and
grasping when we should be generous.

Forgive our sin;
overlook our iniquities; and
redeem us from our own trespasses.

Thank you
for hearing our confession,
forgiving our wrongs, and
healing our wounds.

In the power of your Holy Spirit,
save us from ourselves;
teach us to order our lives according to your word; and
restore our sense of right and wrong
that we might weather the storms of this life.

In Jesus' name, Amen.

9/10/2017

43. Adoration

Almighty God,

We will sing to you a new song,
spreading your praise throughout the world,
proclaiming your name and
telling of your salvation every day.

For you created the universe and
sustain all that is in it.
Your mercy abounds to all
who call on your name.

So let the nations worship God,
the one who reigns!

Worship God and him alone
for his glory and majesty and strength!

Let heaven be glad and rejoice—
let the waters rush and the sea foam;
let it rage;
let the fields praise you;
let the forests sing of your glory.

Before the Lord,
none can stand
for he will judge the earth in righteous and
the people in truth (Ps 96), Amen.

7/9/2017

HEALING

44. Healing from Sin

Oh Lord Almighty,

Teach us
to humble ourselves,
to live into your call, and
to be your people in thought, word, and deed.

Teach us
to pray aright,
to seek your face, and
to turn from all wickedness,
especially the wickedness of racism.

Hear our prayer—
be not far away,
but especially near
when our hearts are weary.

Let not our youth or our old age
become an excuse for sin.

In the power of your Holy Spirit,
forgive our sin and
heal our land.

In Jesus' precious name, Amen

9/3/2017

45. Healing

Holy Father, Great Physician, Spirit of Truth,

We praise you, Lord,
for you are good—
your mercy extends to us
even as we are ungrateful and undeserving.

We confess
that your mercy is infinitely greater than ours
that we seldom practice forgiveness and
are frequently in need of it.

Do not hold our sin against us
nor let our iniquity bind us, for Jesus' sake.

We give thanks
for the gifts of family, friends in Christ, and
the many blessings in this life.

Break the chains
that bind our hearts and minds—
the pain,
the curses passed through the generations, and
the bad blood that has accumulated
in a life marred by selfishness, envy, greed, and malice.

In our hour of need,
may we turn to you,
not only for our own sake,
but for the sake of those around us.

Cleanse our hearts
that our bodies might also be healed.

May the doctors be perplexed by our healing and
the nurses shocked by our change of heart—
that your goodness and mercy
would be obvious to all.

In Jesus' precious name, Amen.

3/18/2018

46. Casting Out Dark Shadows

Almighty Father,

We praise you
for your love in creating us in your image and
confess that we are unworthy of this high honor.

Thank you
for the faith to endure suffering—
knowing that until you return in glory
*"suffering produces endurance, and endurance
produces character, and character produces hope."*
(Rom 5:3–4)

Knowing also
that for those whose faith is weak
you are ever-present and
have granted to us dominion
over every creeping thing. (Gen 1:28)

We claim this promise
in the strong name of Jesus Christ,
who died on the cross and
was raised from the dead.

In Jesus' name—
we bind every dark shadow,
break the power of every curse,
every abuse, and every evil thought.
We cast every spirit of self-destruction and
resignation into the fiery pit.

We raise up the cross and declare:
no more, be gone.

Fill every heart with your Holy Spirit,
that lives might echo your light and joy.
May every child confess
that Jesus is Lord until you return in glory.

In his holy name, Amen.

6/24/2018

47. Healing, Comfort, and Deliverance

God Almighty, Great Physician, Holy Spirit,

We praise you
for your goodness in granting us life,
which we often take for granted,
living as if tomorrow was always promised,
but knowing that it is not.

Break the power of sin over our lives—
forgive us for our presumptions,
for our neglect of giving thanks, and
for living selfishly for ourselves,
as though we were worthy.

Thank you
for your eternal presence,
your healing touch, and
for sending others to comfort us in our hour of need.

Break our bondage to worthless idols—
heal our broken bodies,
our troubled spirits, and
our damaged relationships,
for your name's sake.

In the power of your Holy Spirit,
send us doctors to offer your healing touch and
nurses to offer your comfort in lonely hours.

Grant us strength for the day;
grace for those we meet; and
peace in a troubled world
that we might rest only in you,

Healing

this day and every day.

In Jesus' precious name, Amen.

1/29/2017

48. Co-Dependence

Loving Father,

We praise you
for the many blessings of this life—
for family, good health, and your provisions,
for we know that they are gifts
that are given to some and
withheld from many.

We confess
that we are unworthy of your generosity and
do not always act like your children,
harboring unclean thoughts, and
acting out of unsavory motivations.

We thank you
for remembering us in our fallen state and
raising us from death to life in Jesus Christ
by the power of your Holy Spirit.

Thank you
for our freedom
to live in the love of Christ.

Remember also those
who do not live in your light—
turn their hearts
through the power of your Holy Spirit and
grant them the faith to accept your mercy.

Let them not live in fear
depending on the strength of others,
but grant them legs to stand on

that they might be whole again.

In the strong name of Jesus Christ
who died on the cross and
was raised from the dead,
we come against any family curses and
cast out any lingering spirits of
fear, abuse, guilt, shame, addiction,
condemnation, territory, or disease.

We bind and cast out
the spirit of the child.

We ask the Holy Spirit to enter this person's heart and bind them to Christ Jesus, now and always.

In Jesus' precious name, Amen.

6/17/2018

HOLIDAYS

49. New Year's 2017

Merciful Father, Light of the World, Spirit of Truth,

Thank you for the gift of life,
the time to enjoy it, and
the many blessings
that we take for granted.

Forgive us for wasting your gifts—
for the sins that we willfully commit, and
for the good things that we forget to do.

Have mercy on us.

Cast out
the demons that torment us,
the desires that demean us, and
the spirits that hide us from the truth.

Be especially near.

Help us to reflect on our weaknesses—
our sinful behavior and
our neglectful hearts.

Grant us strength
to meet the challenges of the New Year and
the grace to extend our blessings to those around us.

In Jesus's precious name, Amen

12/31/2017

50. Lent

Holy Father,

In the night,
I hear your voice and
it gives me comfort—
knowing that you are near and
I need not fear the darkness.

In the morning,
I see your light and
I find strength for the day—
knowing that you have ordained it and
I need only play my part.

In the afternoon,
I hear your footsteps behind me and
do not feel alone,
for your hedge of protection is strong and reliable.

In the evening,
I feel your warmth and
take comfort in rest—
for you rested on the seventh day and
declared it to be holy.

I confess
in the shadow of your cross
that my good works are filthy rages in your sight—
you are my only righteousness.

Forgive me
for the unholy things that I had done and
the righteous things that I failed to do,

that I might never leave your presence.

In the power of your Holy Spirit,
grant me the strength
to forgive the sins of those around me.

In Jesus' precious name, Amen.

3/5/2017

51. Lent 2018

Merciful Father,

Have mercy on me, oh Lord, during Lent,
the forty days of preparation for Holy Week and Easter.

In the power of your Holy Spirit,
open my eyes as I pray and
unstop my ears—
may my heart and mind
reflect on your infinite mercy.

For mercy defines who you are and
informs your other attributes—
For you are: *"merciful and gracious, slow to anger, and abounding in steadfast love and faithfulness."* (Exod 34:6)

Because you are merciful,
you offer us grace;
you are slow to anger;
you abound in steadfast love;
you display your faithfulness.

We especially see your mercy
in the death and resurrection of your son and
our savior, Jesus Christ.

Bless us now with the strength
to abstain from sin and reflect on Easter.

In Jesus' precious name, Amen.

3/11/2018

52. Church Workers at Easter

Almighty Father,

Bless the workers in your church
with your special presence during this holiday season.

Grant them strength to get their work done,
grace to extend your blessings to those they serve, and
the peace that passes all understanding.

Give them more hours in every day and
times of silence to listen for your voice
that their work will reflect your glory and
more people will call you father.

In the power of your Holy Spirit,
revive us, your church.

In Jesus' tender name, Amen.

4/8/2018

53. Easter

Blessed Lord Jesus,

We praise you
for remembering us in our celebrations and joy,
in our loneliness and fear,
in spite of who we were, are, or will ever be.

We confess
that we forget you—
when things go well,
when pain becomes overwhelming, and
when we ought to know better.

We give thanks for Easter—
a time of resurrection, new life, and abundant possibilities,
a time when we know that we are not alone, but are loved,
a time that begins a season of waiting for your Holy Spirit.

In the power of the Holy Spirit,
we ask for eyes that see and ears that hear—
that we might share in your new life and
see the Father's love in and through you. Amen.

3/19/2017

54. Mom

Dear Heavenly Father,

Thank you for moms.

Mom, the one who always came running
when I got into trouble as a child and
has modeled your presence in my life ever since.

The one who always listens to me,
even when I make no sense and
go on and on.

The one who says nice things about me,
even when I feel just awful and beat myself up.

Watch over and protect my mom,
especially when I am not around.

Teach me to emulate her patience,
especially when I don't want to.

In the power of your Holy Spirit,
help me to be a better son,
like your son and
our savior, Jesus Christ. Amen

5/14/2017

55. Mother's Day 2018

Heavenly Father,

Thank you for my mother
who brought me into this world,
raised and encouraged me.

Thank you
for your ongoing presence and encouragement.

Be especially present in her life today.

Though many years have passed between us,
may each day be a blessing.

In the power of your Holy Spirit,
may she continue to walk with you and
serve you as well as she has served me.

In Jesus' precious name, Amen.

5/13/2018

56. Father's Day

Heavenly Father:

We praise you
for being a loving father—
who is a good provider,
who is always available,
who loves us even when we are unlovable.

We confess
that we are frequently none of these things—
not especially loving,
not available when we should be,
not able to see beyond our own needs.

We thank you
for the example of Jesus Christ—
who demonstrated sacrificial love,
who remained available at the cost of his own life,
who loved the many unlovable people
whom we typically ignore.

In the power of your Holy Spirit
give us the desire and the ability
to love, to be available, and
to see beyond our own needs.

In Jesus' name, Amen.

6/25/2017

57. Thanksgiving

Oh Dear Lord,

We give thanks
for creating us—
may we reflect your goodness,
cherish our families, and
grow as stewards of your creation.

As your image bearers,
help us to honor you in all that we do.

We give thanks
for our salvation in Jesus Christ and
for his life, his teaching, his sacrifice,
his death, and resurrection.

May we share this blessing with all those around us.

We give thanks
for the presence of your Holy Spirit,
who sustains us, provisions us, empowers us,
heals our wounds, and
grants us good gifts to share.

In Jesus' name, Amen.

11/12/2017

58. *Evangelists*

Almighty Father, Beloved Son, Holy Spirit,

We give thanks
that you bless us
with your word and your presence,
with family, good health, and
with our many needs.

May we model your mercy
by blessing those around us,
that your love would be multiplied
over and over again.

Go with us now
as we reach out to the lives of those around us
in word and in deed,
especially in this Advent season.

Grant us
strength for the day;
grace for those we meet; and
peace.

In Jesus' precious name, Amen.

12/11/2016

59. Advent 2016

Compassionate and Merciful Lord,

We approach your throne of grace
in this advent season with heavy hearts,
confident that the Christ child will soon arrive and
equally confident that we will not be ready.

Have mercy on us.

Forgive our sins this year—
sins knowingly committed,
sins committed in your full view
that burden our hearts.

Have mercy on us.

Open our hearts
to those less fortunate than us,
those whose children may be hungry,
be they near or far away.

Have mercy on us.

Prepare us for the arrival of your son,
yet a child, unwanted, unknown to the world.

Through the power of your Holy Spirit,
heal our wounds,
visible and hidden,
that joy might return and
we might be ready for your coming.

In Jesus precious name, Amen.   12/4/2016

60. Advent 2017

Most Merciful Father,

Draw me near to you, oh Lord, of joyful times!

Let me bless you and praise your name—
"Wonderful Counselor, Mighty God,
Everlasting Father, Prince of Peace." (Isa 9:6)

For you have written your law on our hearts (Jer 31:33) and given us a new song. (Ps 98)

In what other season do we have so much joy?

We give thanks
through the power of your Holy Spirit and
in Jesus' name, Amen.

12/3/2017

61. Christmas 2016

Heavenly Father,

We give thanks
for your special presence with us at Christmas
when you came to us, lived among us, suffered with us, and
made us members of your family.

Such a gift! Such a surprise! So undeserved!

We confess
that we desperately need you,
the light of the world.

Lights on a tree,
lights in the yard,
lights in the mall,
all pall next to your light.

Let us not forget;
leave us not alone;
be ever nearer each passing day.

In the power of your Holy Spirit,
help us to look around us each day and
extend your light even further.

Through Jesus' special name, Amen.

12/25/2016

62. Christmas 2017

Father of all mercy,

Thank you
for sending Jesus Christ into our world
while we were yet sinners. (Rom 5:8)

Though darkness filled our world,
you sent us light. (Gen 1:3; Luke 1:4)

You and you alone have given us
faith, hope, dignity, and the example of love.

In the power of your Holy Spirit,
restore in us the joy of your creation,
as that day with the birth of a baby,

In the name of Jesus Christ, our Lord, Amen.

12/24/2017

FAMILY

63. Family

Almighty Father, Beloved Son, Holy Spirit,

We give thanks for the gift of family.

For those who went before us
who brought us together,
made us who we are and
led us to faith in you.

For the sacrifices of our parents
who brought us into this world,
for the time that we have shared,
for the children who you have given us.

For our spiritual family,
which is the church,
where we live and grow and
have our being.

For the blessings
that you have showered on us
out of your love for us and
the perfect example of love
that only you provide.

For all these things,
we give thanks,
all honor and glory.

In Jesus' name, Amen.

11/27/2016

64. Family 2017

Heavenly Father,

Thank you for our families—
the ones who raise and care for us,
when we are small and weak, and
cannot care for ourselves.

Break the power of evil words and
weak DNA to hurt our family.

Cast out sin and
the power of evil among us.

Bless our parents, our siblings,
our aunts and uncles, and grandparents
with faith and wisdom and
your Holy Spirit
that their example may reflect Christ's teaching
to the whole community.

Through the power of your Holy Spirit,
may their lips always profess thanks, and
may we care for them
even more dearly than they have cared for us.

In Jesus' name. Amen.

8/6/2017

65. Kids

Almighty Father,

We praise you
for creating us, male and female,
in your image (Gen 1:27)
so that in Christ
"there is neither Jew nor Greek,
there is neither slave nor free,
there is no male and female." (Gal 3:28)

We confess
that we have not always
lived into your image or even wanted to.

We give thanks
that you have not given up on us,
but sent Christ to show us how to live,
ransomed us from our own sinful folly, and
given us the hope of salvation and
eternal life with you.

We pray
that our kids will remember the lessons
that we so painfully learned.

In the power of your Holy Spirit,
grant us the strength to continue living another year,
the grace to reach out to those around us, and
the peace that passes all understanding. (Phil 4:7)

In Jesus' name, Amen.

1/7/2018

66. Elderly Parents

Holy Father,

All praise and glory be to you
for providing us faithful parents—
role models to guide us through the wilds of life
before we could tell our left hand from the right.

Thank you
for their care, sacrifice, and wisdom—
may we be so caring,
so willing to sacrifice, and so wise.
Forgive us when we are not!

Be with them when we are unable
that they would never be alone;
protect them from those
who prey on the elderly,
from unexpected accidents, and
from needless worry.

In the power of your Holy Spirit,
grant us the strength and
wisdom to be worthy children and loving caregivers
that we might enjoy our remaining times together and
provide a role model to the young.

In Jesus precious name, Amen.

1/21/2018

INTERCESSION

67. Election 2016

Almighty God, Creator of Heaven and Earth,

We give thanks
for our home, America the Beautiful,
which you have blessed from sea to shining sea—
with the rule of law and
the hope for a future;
with opportunities beyond measure—
for education,
for health care,
for meaningful work, and
for worshiping you without persecution.

In this land of plenty,
may we humbly remember—
that our greatest gift is your presence and
that our blessings come from you.

Place your hedge of protection around us
as we elect a new president.

Guide our decisions.

In the land of the free,
may we humbly remember—
that you are in control and
that presidents come and go
at your bidding, not ours.

In the power of your Holy Spirit,
heal our hearts, inspire our minds and guide our hands—
that we might grow closer to you each day and

that revival might begin with us and sweep across this land.

In Jesus' precious name, Amen.

11/6/2016

68. Innocent Students

Merciful Father,

Have mercy on the innocent young people
who are being gunned down too often in our schools.

Banish the images of horror,
of bodies bloodied,
of students running with their hands in the air, and
of stories of what might have been.

Create in us clean hearts, O God, and
renew a right spirit within us;
cast us me not away from your presence; and
take not your Holy Spirit from us. (Ps 51:10–11)

Let us not bend our hearts
with electronic fantasies of power or
hide ourselves from those around us.

But in the power of your Holy Spirit—
"be Thou our vision,
O Lord of our hearts;
naught be all else to us,
save that Thou art;
Thou our best thought,
by day or by night;
waking or sleeping,
Thy presence our light".[1]

In Jesus' precious name. Amen.   6/10/2018

---

1 https://www.hymnal.net/en/hymn/ns/345.

69. Silent People

Almighty Father,

All praise and honor be yours, Lord,
for bringing caring people into my life;
for I am not an island,
much as I would like to be;
for my freedom in Christ is
to live within the boundaries that you set,
able to resist the compulsions
of my sinful nature.

I confess, Lord,
that I forget to raise my concerns up in prayer and
to pray over the many decisions
that I face each day;
that my sinful desires would destroy me,
were I to yield to them;
that I am totally dependent on your goodness and mercy
every day of my life.

I give thanks
for your Holy Spirit's guidance and provision,
especially for placing many saints in my life.

Help me to remember the silent people—
those forgotten because of their social status—
whose work goes unnoticed
masquerading in products and services
that I barely understand,
but depend on every day.

Bless them;
may I learn to honor them daily.

In Jesus' precious name, Amen.

2/4/2018

70. Teachers

Heavenly Father,

We praise you
for bringing good teachers into our lives.

Teachers who care, are well-trained, and
work tirelessly to help us learn—
teachers better than any child deserves!

Help us to listen to advice and
accept instruction (Prov 19:20) and
teach us to number our days
that we may gain a heart of wisdom. (Ps 90:12)

We confess
that we often tire of learning and
spend too little time on pursuing wisdom.

Thank you
none-the-less for those who labor to instruct us
that we might mature
into people of wisdom and faith, and
not stumble through life
in ignorance for lack of guidance.

In the power of your Holy Spirit,
enlighten our minds and
open our hearts
that we might grow more like you
day by day.

In Jesus' name, Amen. 1/14/2018

71. Persecution

Eternal and Compassionate God,

We thank you, Lord,
for visiting us
when we are afflicted and suffer unjustly;
for you are a God who cares,
who understands our grief, our wounds,
our diseases, our fears.

We lay our afflictions before you
for we cannot bear them alone.

Heal our wounds,
comfort us when we grieve, and
purge our diseases.

Restore us;
redeem us;
save us;
teach us to bind the wounds,
griefs, and diseases of those around us, and
to point them to you.

Teach us
to intercede for the people around us
by our actions and through our prayer.

For you are our God and
we are your people.
You are with us;
you are for us; and

you have given your name to us.

In the power of your Holy Spirit,
let our security reside only in you,
now and always.

In Jesus' name, Amen.

6/18/2017

72. Authors

Almighty father, Author of our Faith, Spirit of Truth,

All glory and honor are yours, Lord,
for you have shown us who you are—
*"a God merciful and gracious, slow to anger, and
abounding in steadfast love and faithfulness."* (Exod 34:6)

You have taught us all things,
as the Psalmist pleads:
*"Lead me in your truth and teach me,
for you are the God of my salvation;
for you I wait all the day long."* (Ps 25:5)

We confess
that we are slow learners and
none are righteous before you. (Ps 143:2)

But we rejoice and give thanks
for the salvation that is ours
through confession of sin and
faith in Jesus Christ. (Rom 10:10)

As the Author of our Faith (Heb 12:2 KJV) and
the Spirit of Truth. (John 15:13)
we ask for your guidance as we write
that we might reflect your image (Gen 1:27)
brightly, boldly, and truthfully each day.

In the power of your Holy Spirit,
guard our hearts and minds
as you guide our hands.

Through Jesus Christ, Amen

73. *Comfort for Those Alone*

Blessed Lord Jesus,

Comfort those who are alone—
with their grief,
in their pain,
with their anguish,
in their poverty,
with memories of years past and
no one to share them with.

Thank you
for the example of someone
who cared about lonely people.

Be especially present in the lives of those
who are alone today—
bring new voices, new faces, and
helping hands into their lives.

In the power of your Holy Spirit,
open our hearts to those around us
that we might truly be sons and daughters of one father.

In your name we pray, Amen.

10/23/2016

74. Those in Peril

Almighty God,

We thank you for
the security of a roof over our heads,
gas to power our heaters, and
power to run our appliances.

Help us to remember those who lack these things.

We thank you
for the mercy of being born in a land of plenty
that gave us food to eat,
clean water to drink, and
sanitary plumbing to use.

Help us to remember those who lack these things.

We thank you
for the protection of honest police,
the care of competent physicians, and
the instruction of educated teachers.

Help us to remember those who lack these things.

Give us discerning minds,
tender hearts, and helping hands,
when we forget who we are and
how you have called us.

In the power of your Holy Spirit,
bridge the gap
between discerning minds and the ones we have,

tender hearts and the ones we have,
helping hands and the ones we have.

Forgive us, heal us, and save us from our gaps.

In Jesus' precious name, Amen.

10/16/2016

75. *Memory Impaired*

Almighty Father,

We praise you
for the company that you bring—
make your presence especially obvious
in lonely evenings and busy mornings,
in hymns of praise and silent moments,
in the dark recesses of our minds and
in light moments of joy.

We confess
that we do not always remember—
be our memory.

We thank you
for the hedge of protection that you offer us—
keep us safe from simple falls,
keep us safe from those who prey on older people,
surround us with people who care.

In the power of your Holy Spirit,
be our light, our song, and our joy, and
our salvation when days draw short.

In Jesus' precious name, Amen.

2/26/2017

76. Traveling Mercies

Almighty Father,

As the Psalmist writes—
where shall I go to escape
from your presence?

If I climb up in the heavens or
dig deep in the earth—
you are with me.

If I fly to the rising sun or
hide under the sea—
even there
you take me by the hand and guide me.

If I think to myself when I sin,
ah ha, the darkness of night hides me,
even the darkness
is like the noon day sun to you. (Ps 139:7–12)

Thank you, Lord,
for being ever near, caring for us—
even when our strength fails us;
even when our minds go blank;
even when we are not our best.

Place your hedge of protection
around the ones we love
as they journey through life, often carelessly, and
bring them back to us again
through the power of your Holy Spirit.

In Jesus' precious name, Amen.   4/2/2017

SEASONS

77. Open Doors

Merciful Father,

Thank you
for the freshness of
a new day, a new week, and a New Year.

When possibilities seem,
within reach and boundless,
like a child who discovers dandelions
for the first time.

Remove the blinders
that limit our vision,
the muffles over our ears, and
the clamp that pinches our noses—
re-invigorate our lost, yet youthful senses.

Bless us
that we might bless those around us.

In the power of your Holy Spirit,
give us open doors
that we can walk through and
never look back.

In Jesus precious name, Amen.

1/8/2017

78. January

Eternal Father, Prince of Peace, Spirit of Truth,

We give thanks
for a month of new possibilities,
not looking back,
not fearing the future,
but focused on the present.

Be especially present,
eternally present,
in our lives here and now.

May we participate in your shalom,
the peace that passes all understanding, and
share it with those around us.

In our sense of peace,
give us the serenity
to examine our thoughts,
our emotions, and our responses,
that they may honor and
be sanctified by your presence,
every hour of each day.

In the power of your Holy Spirit,
may your truth guide us closer to you.

In Jesus' precious name, Amen.

1/15/2017

79. Tulips

Merciful Father,

Bring on the tulips;
I am ready for spring.

Clear out the cobwebs;
open the windows;
pull back the curtains.

Shine your light
into the dark recesses of my mind;
let me hide in the shadows no more—
I want to plant seeds
to watch them grow and
to live in the sunshine of your love.

In the power of your Holy Spirit,
let me enter the garden of your life.

In Jesus' name, Amen.

4/2/2018

80. Spring

Blessed Lord Jesus,

We praise you
for new life;
for not leaving us alone
in the sad graveyards of our sins and limitations;
for planting seeds in the soil of our hearts,
where daffodils can sprout,
grow, and flower unexpectedly
and we can share in your resurrection.

We confess
that we seldom look for you or
welcome you into our busy lives;
seldom model your goodness to our neighbors;
seldom even try to avoid sin
with iniquity being our default setting.

Thank you
for warm spring mornings,
when the sunshine reminds us
that winter is not forever,
strong winds remind us of your Holy Spirit; and
gentle rain reminds us
that you give life to all the earth.

Grant us
strength for the day;
grace for those we meet; and
the peace that passes all understanding.

In the name of the Father, Son, and Holy Ghost, Amen.
3/12/2017

81. Summer

Holy Father,

I praise you
for quiet summer days—
when I do not need to work;
when time stands still and
is a joy to experience; and
when my only worry
is about how to enjoy the day.

Be ever near—
guard my heart and mind; and
teach me to number my days aright. (Ps 90)

In Jesus' name, Amen.

7/2/2017

82. When Daylight Fades

Ever-present Father,

Oh Lord, God of my youth
when days were long and
nights were short,
be especially near now
as twilight approaches and
I feel all alone.

Remind me of
the times we shared,
the beaches we walked, and
the forests we explored—
when each discovery was a blessing to share with you and
with those near me,
when hope was founded on the newest of life and
your constant companionship, and
I did not know how to fear or
what to fear or when to fear,
because everything was fresh, new, and bright
and my candy bag was bigger than me and
I could wear any costume with equal glee.

Oh Lord, God of my elder days
as nights grow longer and
the days slip by,
be especially near
as twilight sneaks up on me and
I feel less energetic.

Guard my heart
in my weaker moments and
bless me with your wisdom,

when my own wisdom seems shallow and
my need ever so great.

Remind me
that we still share time together and
that the freshness of our time
is as vital as the splendor of my youth.

In the power of your Holy Spirit,
provide strong hands to support me
when my own hands fail and
the strength to carry your light
though the darkness
that seems so near.

In Jesus' name, Amen.

10/30/2016

83. Attentiveness

Eternal Father,

The days pass quickly
like leaves changing color before their time.

Where did the summer go?

I am not ready for fall;
I am not ready for brisk winds and shorter days.

Lord, help me to be attentive to the times and seasons—
to lift my gaze from my computer screen,
to listen for the sirens warning me
as emergency vehicles pass in the distance
that I am neither alone,
nor as strong as I might imagine in my dreams.

What was it that I missed
while I struggled in the days of spring and summer
to learn all my lessons and
to earn enough to support a family?

Help me
to embrace the slower pace,
the changing roles,
the weeds that need to be pulled,
the fruit in need of picking
that I have so carelessly planted and
left for others to tend.

Why is it quieter now
when all I remember is commotion,
running, and shouting?

Is it not enough to rest my soul,
to draw nearer to you, and
to not fear empty hours?

Lord, help me to be attentive
to the thoughts, feelings, and people
that for too long seemed only nice to know.

Lord, help me to see your face,
to feel your presence,
to recognize your Spirit's invitation, and
to become more like your Son.

In Jesus precious name, Amen.[1]

10/2/2016

---

[1] Inspired by Leighton Ford, 2008, *The Attentive Life: Discerning God's Presence in All Things*, Downers Grove: IVP Books.

84. Autumn

Almighty Father,

We praise you
as the Alpha and the Omega,
the beginning and the end
of things seen and unseen.

Thank you
for letting us enjoy the breath of life,
spring, summer, autumn, and
the winter to come.

Thank you
especially for your presence,
for in your presence,
there is healing, life, and joy.

Show us
how to disciple in each season of life,
in its newness and fullness,
in its setbacks and victories,
for alone we would perish
as many do,
day after day.

For in each new day is life and joy, learning and maturity,
condemnation and judgment, sickness and death,
but you lead us in your infinite wisdom,
through the power of your Holy Spirit
until we see you face to face.

In Jesus' name, Amen.   11/19/2017

85. Winter

Almighty Father,

I praise you
for your loving kindness,
which you demonstrated on Calvary
with the sacrifice of your son, Jesus Christ.

I praise you
for your faithfulness,
which we witness each morning
in the beauty and warmth of the rising sun.

I confess
that my own kindness flags too often to mention and
I am neither warm nor bright in the morning and
sometimes all day.

Thank you, Lord,
that I am not the center of the universe and
I am not reminded each day
of my weaknesses and cold disposition.

Thank you, Lord,
for the warm house that I live in and
the warm people who keep me safe.

I pray
for warmer weather and
the new life of spring,
which heals the body and
refreshes the soul.

In Jesus' name, Amen.   12/17/2017

86. Stillness of Winter

Resurrection Lord,

Thank you
for the stillness of night and
quiet of winter,
when we can rest alone and
yet not fear—
for fear too often accompanies our lives,
when things do not go as planned and
our lack of control terrorizes us—
death looms near;
friends seem distant; and
sunshine eludes us.

In the midst of our loneliness,
you provide Sabbath—
rest from the busyness;
rest from illness;
rest from our imagined demons.

In the midst of our insecurities,
you offer resurrection—
new life, hope, and purpose
for which we give thanks.

In Jesus' precious name, Amen.

2/19/2017

LAMENTATIONS

87. Covering Prayer

Merciful Father,

Cover me, Lord, with your mercy—
like a morning blanket
when I am not ready to face the day;
when coffee offers no temptation; and
when the sun's warmth seems yet so distant.

I want to be someone else,
somewhere else,
in some other time.

For my life has too many moving parts and
I feel like the scraps of meat being fed into a grinder or
toothpaste being squeezed out of the tube.

Why do I despair; where has my strength gone?

Yet, you, oh Lord, are my hope.

In the power of your Holy Spirit,
draw me especially close today
so the blanket's temptation dissipates and
my coffee beckons.

Grant me the peace
that passes all understanding
in Jesus' precious name, Amen.

5/6/2018

88. *When We are Alone*

Almighty Father,

Reach out to me this morning and
comfort me in my solitude—
lonely, missing one so dear.

I know
that I should not be sad for a life well-lived,
for someone strong
who showed me how to live and
then how to die.

Yet, I am sad,
because it is my turn to be strong and
I do not want to be.

In the power of your Holy Spirit,
grant me time and space and
strength to grieve,
to let tears flow.

For the season at hand is for such.

In Jesus' precious name, Amen.

4/30/2017

89. Dimmer Lights

Heavenly Father,

Prepare our hearts, oh Lord,
for the coming holidays
when we must face
that empty chair,
must answer questions
that intrude too much; and
too much remember
events from a past
that refuses to be history.

Turn down the lights—
let the old music play more gently; and
give me some space
when I seem distant.

In the power of your Holy Spirit—
remind me of your love and
shelter me in your arms again
under Christmas lights.

In Jesus' precious name, Amen.

12/18/2016

90. Grief

God of all Mercy and Compassion,

You are the Alpha and Omega—
the beginning and the end,
the one who was, who is, and
who is to come. (Rev 1:9)

For you created heaven and earth for your glory and
we praise you for their beauty and our creation. (Ps 19)

Make your presence especially known among us today
for our eyes are heavy with tears and
our ears barely hear.

With heavy hearts we, your people, stand before you
confessing our sins and our doubts,
but confident of the love of Christ.

We thank you
for sharing our friend with us
during his season of life.

We praise you
for our friend's compassion,
quiet dignity and devotion to family,
constant smile and companionship, and
daily presence in our lives.

In the power of the Holy Spirit,
grant us a season of grief as life passes.

Open our hearts;
let us cry;

help us feel and
express our loss.

Place your hedge of protection around us as we grieve—
protect our persons and our spirits;
guard our relationships; and
help us keep our jobs.

Let us not have to choose
between expressing our grief and other things.

May our grief be godly grief that leads to salvation,
not worldly grief that leads to sin and death.
(2 Cor 7:10)

In our grieving,
let us be like Job
who did not sin in spite of many afflictions. (Job 1:13–22)

But let us turn to you in our lament,
great giver of life,
to empty our hearts of the pain,
the shame, the guilt, and the grief
so that we might once again
enter your gates with praise.

For we know
that you grieved over Lazarus and
the widow's son, and
raised them both from the dead
even though no words of faith were spoken.
(John 11:1–46; Luke 7:11–17)

May we know
that through Jesus Christ
death does not have the last word.

Let us be like Christ who was raised from death to new life.

Remind us daily that—
"neither death nor life, nor angels nor rulers,
nor things present nor things to come,
nor powers, nor height nor depth,
nor anything else in all creation,
will be able to separate us from the love of God
in Christ Jesus our Lord." (Rom 8:38–39)

By the power of your Holy Spirit,
grant us the strength to turn to you in our grief,
following the example of Jesus at Gethsemane. (Matt 26:3)

Let us live life in view of the resurrection and
the eternal life that is ours in Jesus Christ. (John 3:16)

In the strong name of Jesus we pray. Amen.

8/13/2017

91. Cooler Weather

Almighty Father,

We praise you
for the gift of your Holy Spirit,
who provisions, sustains, and guides us
when cooler heads do not prevail.

We confess
that this has been a long, hot summer,
fires burn in our forests, but also in our hearts.

Thankfully,
you are God and we are not.
You protect us when we act like mythical lemmings—
running off cliffs
when stressed by competition and deprivation.

Teach us
to model ourselves after Jesus Christ,
who taught self-sacrifice and unity
when the world taught war and division.

In the power of your Holy Spirit,
save us from ourselves and
turn our hearts and minds to you.

In Jesus' precious name, Amen.

9/9/2018

STRENGTH

92. Workouts

Merciful Father,

Thank you for each new day—
the chance to witness a new sunrise and
to feel the warm summer breeze,
the opportunity to participate in new life,
to care for the old, and
to experience your pleasure in both.

May your Holy Spirit inhabit this temple,
which is my body (1 Cor 6:19)
all the days of my life.

May I remain a fit custodian—
praying to you
even as I work out in the gym,
swim my laps, and
compete on the field.

Bless my heart
that it might be ever open to the pain of others;
bless my mind
that it might attend to your commandments and
not be seduced by sin;
bless my legs
that they might carry where you would have me go; and
bless my arms
that they might carry the burdens of your children.

Teach me to care for your people
the way that I care for my own body.

Grant me strength for the day,
grace for those I meet, and
the peace that passes all understanding. (Phil 4:7)

In Jesus' precious name. Amen.

3/4/2018

93. Thanks for Quiet Days

Oh dear Lord,

Thank you for quiet days—
when nothing needs to be done,
when the rain seems endless, and
when we can recover from the turbulence of life.

Be especially close;
guard our worn-out hearts; and
keep us from sinning.

In the power of your Holy Spirit,
heal our wounds.

In Jesus' precious name, Amen.

2/11/2018

94. Doldrums

Almighty Father, Beloved Son, Holy Spirit,

Remain especially near to me in the doldrums of life,
when the wind is not in my sails and
the sea seems listless, devoid of life.

Let me not sin out of boredom,
let me not wander into danger
for lack of direction, energy, or inspiration.

Give me the fisherman's sense
of when to cut bait and
when to go fishing.

Let me innovate
when stuck in the middle of a transition,
when the good old days have passed, and
when the future remains uncertain.

Teach me
to number my days aright
that I might a heart of wisdom (Ps 90:12)
that I might live into my baptism each day.

In Jesus' name, Amen

7/30/2017

95. Solitude

Quiet Lord,

All praise and honor be yours
as you announce your presence in silence.

The oceans roar, volcanos explode, and
the storm clouds thunder,
but you sit with us in peace when we are alone,
nurturing the silence of our hearts,
letting our voices be heard
even when we do not speak.

Teach us to be like you.

Do not let us project our anger,
pain, or emptiness on those around us;
do not let our childish insecurities
yield to childish violence.

Let us honor your peace.

Let us mirror your beatitudes
that we might one day
be counted among the saints.

Reach out to us through the power of your Holy Spirit.

In Jesus' name, Amen.

8/27/2017

96. Relief

Almighty Father,

All praise be yours
for you are holy, set apart, and righteous and
you have created us in your image,
with the potential to do great things in your name.

We confess
that we do not desire to be called Christians,
for we have tarnished your image, and
remain unholy, willful, and
polluted by the world.

Yet, we give thanks for the life, death and
resurrection of Jesus Christ, and
the gift of the Holy Spirit.

We ask for strength
to resist the besetting weaknesses and sins
that rob our prayers of power and
limit the fruit of our ministry.

In the power of your Holy Spirit
guard our hearts and minds
that we might run the good race and
be victorious in this life

Through Jesus Christ, our Lord, Amen.

6/4/2017

97. Strength

Holy Father,

I praise you for creating me—
for giving me life and health and
all the many blessings of family.

I confess
that I have not always used time wisely and
not always made the best lifestyle choices.

Thank you
for another day—
I have learned not to take them for granted.

The gift of time is precious to me—
help me to make good use of it, and
to be a faithful steward of it.

Thank you
for good health—
I have learned not to take it for granted.

The gift of health is a prerequisite
for everything else that I do—
help me not to abuse it.

In the power of your Holy Spirit,
I ask for strength—
to make good choices;
to be a witness, a good father, and a loving spouse; and
to deal with all the many challenges of this life—
like an oak that grows straight and tall and sturdy.

In Jesus' name,
for *"I can do all things through him who strengthens me."* (Phil 4:13)

Amen.

5/21/2017

98. Vindication

Heavenly Father,

Vindicate me.

Argue my case before committees
that I cannot attend and
protect me from judgmental people
who look only for weakness and
spin goodness into evil.

You are my trusted friend, my refuge—
why does my testing go on and on?

Defend and deliver me
from the doubts and anxieties
that trouble me and leave me weak—
open to temptations and sins
that I would not choose on my own.

Shower me with your light and truth,
lead me to your presence—
that safe place where I can find rest.

Then, I will know the consolation of your spirit;
find sanctuary for my soul; and
trust in you more fully—
the one who saves and
is worthy of praise. (Ps 43)

Bless me with your vindication
that I might vindicate those around me. (Gen 12:3)

In the power of your Holy Spirit and in Jesus' precious name, Amen.

5/7/2017

99. Living Water

Good Shepherd:

Do not leave me alone in this weary land,
where dust and sand blow in my eyes,
where the heat is good only for raising scorpions,
where I may perish in my own sin and
be cut off from my people, and
where foolish hearts lead people astray. (Rom 1:21)

Strike the rock
that is my heart with your staff
that my heart may become a wellspring of life and,
through your Holy Spirit,
bring forth springs of living water
from which many may drink. (Exod 17:6)

In Jesus' name, Amen.

4/9/2017

ABOUT

Author Stephen W. Hiemstra lives in Centreville, VA with Maryam, his wife of more than thirty years. Together, they have three grown children.

Stephen worked as an economist for twenty-seven years in more than five federal agencies, where he published numerous government studies, magazine articles, and book reviews. He wrote his first book, *A Christian Guide to Spirituality* in 2014. In 2015, he translated and published a Spanish edition, *Una Guía Cristiana a la Espiritualidad*. In 2016, he wrote a second book, *Life in Tension*, which also focuses on Christian spirituality. In 2017, he published a memoir, *Called Along the Way*. In 2018, he published an ebook compilation of his first three books, *Spiritual Trilogy*.

Stephen has a Masters of Divinity (MDiv, 2013) from Gordon-Conwell Theological Seminary in Charlotte, NC. His doctorate (PhD, 1985) is in agricultural economics from Michigan State. He studied in Puerto Rico and Germany, and speaks Spanish and German.

Correspond with Stephen at T2Pneuma@gmail.com or follow his blog at http://www.T2Pneuma.net.

www.ingramcontent.com/pod-product-compliance
Lightning Source LLC
Chambersburg PA
CBHW070042230426
43661CB00005B/729